Introduction

POEMS OF FAITH *is our eleventh volume. It includes inspirational poetry on themes of prayer, joy, love and peace.*

It is our hope that this volume will lead the reader on to new spiritual pathways in order to enjoy a stronger and more enriched faith.

May it bring hope and courage in the midst of life's struggles, and joy and serenity in the ordinary moments of life.

Our special thanks go to our ever faithful and generous contributing poets. We also wish to thank the publishers who have permitted us to use some of their poems in this book.

"Keep-A-Goin" by Frank L. Stanton from the book LINES TO LIVE BY published by Thomas Nelson Inc. Used by permission.

Salesian Missions wishes to thank those who have given their kind permission to reprint material included in this book. Every effort has been made to give proper acknowledgements. Any omissions or errors are deeply regretted, and the publisher, upon notification, will be pleased to make necessary corrections in subsequent editions.

Poems of Faith

from the
Salesian Collection

Compiled and Edited
by Sara Tarascio

Illustrated by
Paul Scully
Frank Massa
and
Russell Bushée

CONTENTS

Blessings Come in Many Guises

When troubles come
  and things go wrong.
And days are cheerless
  and nights are long.
We find it so easy
  to give in to despair
By magnifying
  the burdens we bear–

We add to our worries
  by refusing to try
To look for "the rainbow"
  in an overcast sky–
And the blessing God sent
  in a "darkened disguise"
Our troubled hearts
  fail to recognize,
Not knowing God sent it
  not to distress us
But to strengthen our faith
  and redeem us and bless us.

Helen Steiner Rice

Used with permission of
The Helen Steiner Rice Foundation
Suite 2100 Atrium Two
221 E. Fourth Street
Cincinnati, OH 45202

After the Clouds

After every cloud burst
. . . rays of sun come shining through,
After every parching drought
. . . is seen some morning dew.
After every thunder storm
. . . there is a peaceful calm,
After every bitter cold
. . . there's felt a springy warm.
After every tear is shed
. . . a smile soon comes in view,
After friends have loved and gone
. . . there comes some friends anew.
After some dream that you've had
. . . has failed and slipped your grasp,
A new dream soon will take its place
. . . with hope that you can clasp.
After every heartache that
. . . is shed in tears of grief,
Comes the loving hand of God
. . . that offers sweet relief.

Betty Purser Patten

7

Seeds of Hope

When the world is upside down,
Brush away the tears, the frown,
Say a little prayer, and soon
A ray of hope will conquer gloom.
Our lot is easier to bear
When we talk to God in prayer,
And like a beacon shining bright
Prayer will soothe the grievous plight.
Tales of woe, like useless weeds
Serve no purpose, but the seeds
That enable us to cope
Are the prayers of faith and hope.

Elsie Natalie Brady

Soliloquy

I've watched seasons come and go,
seen the long-stemmed roses grow,
watched a robin build her nest
and held an infant to my breast . . .

I've seen a sunrise on the shore
and heard a lion's majestic roar,
watched a sunset in the west,
seen some loved-ones laid to rest . . .

I've seen rainbows in the sky,
seen Niagara and mountains high,
saw a pharoah's wondrous tomb,
the desert cactus in full bloom . . .

I have sailed the oceans blue,
walked barefoot in morning dew,
shed a tear for absent friends
and said a prayer to make amends . . .

I have lived a fulfilled life,
had a kind loving wife;
I'll face death without regret . . .
because the best is coming yet!

Clay Harrison

My Eternal Debt

What do I owe the Lord
   For His countless gifts to me?
How can I thank Him for
   The precious gift to see
The wonders of this world
   In colors, warm and bright,
The sunrise and the sunset,
   And the moon and stars at night . . .

What do I owe the Lord
   For the blessed gift to hear
The sounds, the songs and music,
   And voices, loud and clear,
The Angelus bell at noon,
   The evening call to prayer,
And appreciation of
   The stillness in the air . . .

What do I owe the Lord
    For the comforting gift to feel
The warmth of a helping hand
    Whose touch may help to heal
An ache or a broken heart,
    Or wipe away the tears,
That only a friend can know
Who loved you through the years . . .

I seldom talk about
    These blessings given me,
The list goes on and on,
    How grateful can I be?
Does all this have a price,
    A debt that grows and grows?
How large a debt I owe–
Now only heaven knows!

                Hedwig Wroblewski

11

Praise Him!

Praise Him in the morning
When dewdrops hug each flower.
Praise Him in the noontime
When there breaks a sudden shower.

Praise Him in the twilight
When the birds fly home to nest.
Praise Him in the dark of night
When all the world's at rest.

Praise Him! Praise Him!
Give Him exaltation.
Praise Him! Praise Him!
Sing in adoration.

Jeri Sweany

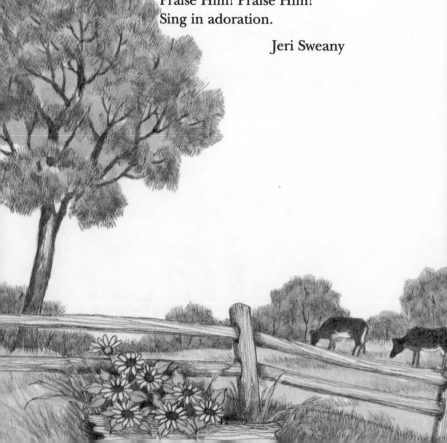

Moods

I kick up the leaves that cover the ground,
Or crunch them beneath my feet;
I find the world a delightful place,
Enjoy everyone I meet.
Yet tomorrow may bring another mood,
My smile may have faded away,
The rain may dampen the once crisp leaves,
And my tears may dampen the day.
There are times of joy, and times of sorrow,
For we can't know only the one,
But on dark days we must keep in mind,
We'll soon rediscover the sun.

Dorothy Niederberger

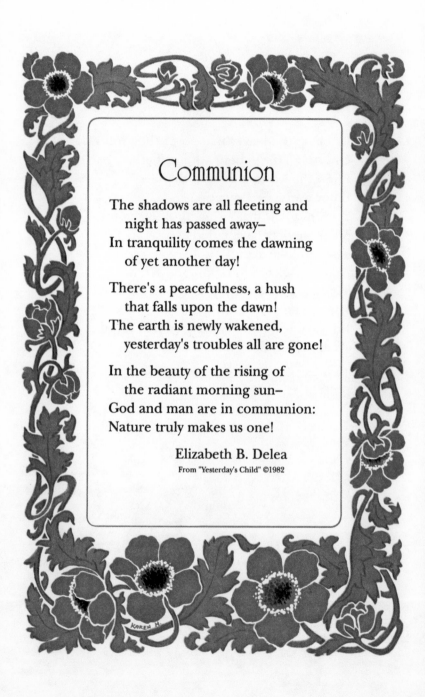

Communion

The shadows are all fleeting and
　　night has passed away–
In tranquility comes the dawning
　　of yet another day!

There's a peacefulness, a hush
　　that falls upon the dawn!
The earth is newly wakened,
　　yesterday's troubles all are gone!

In the beauty of the rising of
　　the radiant morning sun–
God and man are in communion:
Nature truly makes us one!

Elizabeth B. Delea

From "Yesterday's Child" ©1982

Sometimes

Sometimes I'm weak and weary,
    unable to perform,
But my outlook is cheery
    despite the pain and storm.

Sometimes I bend, about to break,
    with sorrows I can't bear ...
Sometimes I cry myself awake
    when no one sees me there.

Sometimes I fear the things I love
    when things don't go my way
Because my faith in God above
    subsides when I don't pray.

Sometimes I'm weak; sometimes I'm strong–
    but God remains the same
And helps me get where I belong
    and makes me glad I came.

Clay Harrison

Rendezvous

I cannot do my work today,
A butterfly is on the fence,
And though I try to concentrate,
I've given up the dull pretense.
How can I think of anything,
When skies are blue and clouds are white,
And crystal waters ripple so,
And little forest trails invite?

I have a rendezvous to keep,
With long-awaited spring this year.
Oh, do not scold me if I seem,
A little absent-minded, dear!

There is a sunny, windblown hill,
Just waiting there for me to climb.
Pack up a lunch and come with me,
There'll never be a better time!

Look how the ivy hugs the wall,
See how the squirrels run and play!
I am a miser who cannot
Afford to waste a single day!
Oh, can't you feel it everywhere?
Impossible, it's only me,
Caught up within the age-old charm,
Of springtime's flowered sorcery!

Grace E. Easley

My Soul Has Wings

Take me to that higher place of peace
Where gravity and tides have lost their stay,
Lift me up above the noise and haste of life
To realms of solitude far, far away.
My soul has wings and longs to rise above
To dwell in peace with God's eternal love.

Margaret Loyd Rockwood

To A Special Friend

Your friendship is the golden sun
that warms the road of life,
and lightens every step I take
beneath my care and strife.
It is the shelter in the storm,
the lighthouse by the sea
that reaches out in time of need
to gently rescue me.
It is the rainbow sparkling fair,
the freshness of the spring.
It is the lilting melody
that sets my heart to sing.
It is the peaceful shady glen
where quiet rivers flow,
the beauty of the morning skies,
the sunset's brilliant glow.
Your friendship is the happy trail
that leads to dreams come true
and I thank God for giving me
a special friend like you!

Beverly J. Anderson

Count Your Blessings

However much I have to do,
   However hard I strive,
I always tell myself that I
   Am glad to be alive.

My heart is grateful for the sun
   That keeps my body warm;
And for the comforts of this earth
Against whatever storm.

I have my friends to cheer me up
   And books to read at night

With boundless beauty to behold,
   Whenever stars are bright.

I have enough to eat and drink,
   And clothes enough to wear;
A normal mind and healthy lungs
   To breathe the best of air.

So why should I object when I
   Have this my job to do,
As long as I have everything
   To help me see this through?

James J. Metcalfe

Divine Guidance

I have so much to tell the world,
But where shall I begin
About how God fed the little birds
And calmed the raging wind.

His love so pure, so rich, so sweet
Engulfs the soul of him
Who cares enough to wait for Christ
And knows He cares for them.

Life has no problem, big or small,
That our Savior does not share
He ever watches o'er our lives
Our every burden, he will bear.

Thy troubled way, thy darkest day
His caring light will illuminate
His joy, His peace are ever near
Wait on the Lord, my soul, Wait!

                    Rose M. Gaines

God Is Love

God is love,
What a wonderful thought;
His love's all around us
Just see what He's wrought.

Beautiful trees,
Blue skies above;
Birds and their songs
All music of love.

Flowers resplendent
With fragrance so rare;
Soft rains to nourish them
All His loving care.

Clear, sparkling water,
Refreshing and bright;
Soft rays of sunshine
To give the earth light.

Then in the evening,
When dark shadows fall;
The moon and the stars
Shine out over all.

How can we doubt
God's loving care;
Just look around you
God's everywhere.

    Ruth Moyer Gilmour

Early Morning

When I arise at early morning
Just before the day begins,
I take time to talk to Jesus
As a friend will talk with friends.

There's a certain peace at daybreak
Just when birds begin their songs,
That's conducive to a prayer life
One can't find in bustling throngs.

God is close to me at all times
And His presence always near,
Yet, there's solitude in morning
When my mind and thoughts are clear.

Every day demands its toiling
And I, too, must do my share,
But it seems to all go better
When I start each day in prayer.

It's so wonderful to wake up
After sleeping in His care,
For the moment I'm awakened
I can feel His presence there.

God's not limited to hours
God's not limited to days,
But He seems to bless the morning
For each child who kneels and prays.

You can make one great investment
That will pay rich dividends,
Just begin the day with Jesus
And He'll be there when it ends.

                    Betty Purser Patten

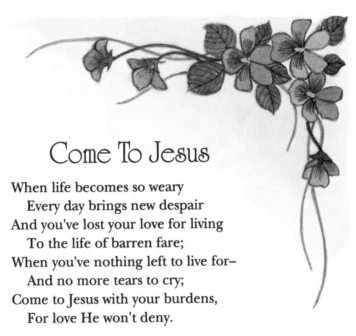

Come To Jesus

When life becomes so weary
   Every day brings new despair
And you've lost your love for living
   To the life of barren fare;
When you've nothing left to live for–
   And no more tears to cry;
Come to Jesus with your burdens,
   For love He won't deny.

He is waiting to embrace you–
   Just a simple prayer away–
And to fill your heart with gladness
   To endear your night and day,
For He knows of all you've suffered,
   In your journeys through the years,
And He knows of faiths you've vanished
   To your struggles and your tears.

Come to Jesus and His comforts–
   Within calling of your cry;
Let Him grant new loves, for sharing,
   And new faiths to journey by;
Let Him give your life new meaning
   And uplift you from despair.
Come to Him–who waits to help you–
   At the moment of your prayer.

              Michael Dubina

A Thought For Today

How little do I know
   as I trudge along each day
   what obstacles will bar my path
   or what blessings my come my way.

How little do I know, but
   how great is my faith in Him,
   that I can brush away any tears
   and struggle on again.

Yes, how little do I know,
   of what tomorrow may be,
   but this I know, that He is near
   and He will take care of me.

                Virginia Luers

In Thankfulness

So much I sought in toil and prayer
Beyond the surge of thirst and hunger,
I had no thought You would provide
Most human needs when I was younger.

I lacked the faith the dawn would bring
A second chance in stony blindness.
How could I know that You would send
This Miracle of love and kindness?

Thank you, dear Lord, for daily blessings,
The rain-filled clouds that nourish birth,
Promised sunrise, abundant harvest
Born in the bosom of the earth.

Give me a thankful heart to share all
Your gifts sublime and commonplace,
And may those passing see Your presence,
Your living image on my face.

Maurice V. Bochicchio

The Flowering Dogwood

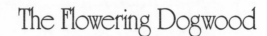

Flowering Dogwood. . . oh, meaning-filled tree,
Laden with blossoms and unfolding leaves,
Humbly you stand in a niche in our yard
Unknowingly spreading your beauty afar . . .
Yellow crown centers and blossom ends scarred,
Twigs indescribably twisted and gnarled;
What breath-taking beauty as my mind's absorbed
In the meaningful legend it tells of our Lord.

Loise Pinkerton Fritz

Thoughts of Spring

Who can feel the touch of springtime,
Who can hear the lark's sweet song,
Who can be caressed by sunshine,
Watch cute lambs skip along …

Who can see the hills green splendor,
Who can thrill to blossomed trees,
Who can watch a tulip opening,
Smell the lilacs on the breeze …

Who can gaze at mauve-clad mountains,
Who can view the vast blue sky,
Who can walk 'mid flowered meadows,
Hear a babbling brook rush by …

Who can know the joys of springtime
And not see the Master's Hand?
Who can doubt when all of nature
Spells God's Name across the land?

Beverly J. Anderson

The Wooden Chapel

High upon a mountain
For all the world to see
Stands a wooden chapel
Beside a tall oak tree.
People come from miles around
To sit and pray awhile,
Life's been hard on all of them
Yet here they wear a smile.
All the hardships that they face
Make days seem really long,
Yet they find the time to pray
And even sing a song.
The paint was white, so long ago
And now it's turning grey,
But through the windows, the sun shines bright
Each and every day.

In the steeple, the bell is cracked
No more can it be rung ...
Still there's peace, and hope for all
That take the time to come.
The chapel's old, it is not grand
It doesn't have to be.
What's in our hearts, is all that counts
And that's what God will see.

Edward Aymar

Sowing Love

Flowers blooming row by row
Delight the soul and eye,
And other gardens can be sown
That also beautify.
Plant a row of kindness,
A row of helpful deeds;
Plant a row to give away
To fill somebody's needs;
Plant a row of thoughtfulness,
A row or two of love–
And you will have a garden
That will rival those above!

Alice Joyce Davidson

From the book "Because I Love You"
Copyright © 1982 by Alice Joyce Davidson
Used by permission of
Fleming H. Revell Company

A Secret Place

Sometimes I need a secret place
   to be alone with God,
Where I can trace, by His sweet grace
   the treasures in His word.
I need that very secret place
   much more than I can tell,
To quietly listen to His voice
   and hear Him say, "All's well."
I need to search and ferret out
   some promise I must claim,
And pray it down from Heaven
   in my blessed Savior's name.
God honors all His promises
   if only we'll believe,
In secret, I ask what I may
   and openly receive.
I need those precious moments, that
   time can't hedge upon,
Just moments I can call my own
   before my Father's throne.
I need that secret audience
   where "two shall meet as one,"
And know that all my prayers are heard
   before my Father's throne.

Betty Purser Patten

True Riches

If all the world were yours to win
And all the wealth and land therein–
If coffers heaped with golden store
Would line your walls and gilt your door
If men would loudly sing your praise
And children would bedeck your ways,
You still would be a beggared lot
If honor somehow was forgot.

If you had naught but daily bread,
A humble cot, a path which led
To where your friends and loved ones wait
With eager smile and open gate–
If none but friends e'er hear your name,
If you are ne'er to taste of fame–
But if self-respect is your creed,
You are a millionaire, indeed.

When I Can't Sleep

When I couldn't sleep
I used to count sheep,
As I tossed on my restless bed,

But since I've known Him
I quietly lie
And talk to the Shepherd instead.

And I pray for the sheep
Who have gone astray,
And ask Him to tenderly hold

The little sick lambs,
So torn by the way,
And bring them back to the fold.

And He whispers to me
As I softly repeat
Sweet promises found in His word,

And my burdens grow less
As I ask Him to bless,
For I know that the Shepherd
   has heard!

      Alice Hansche Mortenson

Keep in Touch

It's always good to keep in touch,
With those who are away,
To let them know they're thought about,
And loved, from day to day.
It only takes a moment,
For a letter or a call,
To be remembered is a thing
That's precious to us all.

And the dear Lord is no different,
How much He loves to hear
The on-the-run "Hello, Lord",
Or the chatty type of prayer.
It's never hard to reach Him,
Whatever may befall,
We've only but to think of Him,
And He can hear us all.

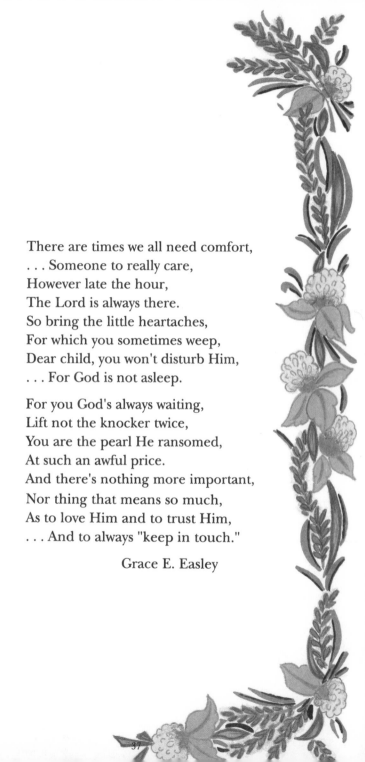

There are times we all need comfort,
. . . Someone to really care,
However late the hour,
The Lord is always there.
So bring the little heartaches,
For which you sometimes weep,
Dear child, you won't disturb Him,
. . . For God is not asleep.

For you God's always waiting,
Lift not the knocker twice,
You are the pearl He ransomed,
At such an awful price.
And there's nothing more important,
Nor thing that means so much,
As to love Him and to trust Him,
. . . And to always "keep in touch."

Grace E. Easley

Jesus Waits

Lonesome is that weary heart
   That beats in life, alone,
And cries for love to light its way
   And show the journey home;
But it is sad, that this should be–
   For any heart to bear–
For Jesus waits, with gifts of love,
   To answer every prayer.

He knows the sadness in a heart
   That weeps for want of love
And cries for light to show the way
   From earth to life, above,
But He cannot reach out with love–
   To comfort one's despair–
Unless the heart, that cries for love,
   Comes unto Him, in prayer.

Michael Dubina

Pray for Hope

Hope is our strongest tool in life
Stronger than faith itself
Or any other implement
That may adorn our shelf.
So dead-end and so blind would be
The alley where we grope,
Unless along the path of life
We always had some hope.
It is a gift from God to us
While we are on this earth,
Our inspiration constantly
To be of better worth.
Without it we would walk with death,
Despair, defeat and fear
And pass the sign,
"Abandon hope . . . All you who enter here."
So let us pray to God that we
May keep our hope alive
And give His grace to reach the goal
For which our souls would strive.

James J. Metcalfe

Choose Carefully

A careless word may kindle strife
A cruel word may wreck a life.
A bitter word may hate instill
A brutal word may smite and kill.

A gracious word may smooth the way
A joyous word may light the day.
A timely word may lessen stress
A loving word may heal and bless.

After the Winter . . .

Springtime is a season
   Of hope and joy and cheer.
There's beauty all around us
   To see and touch and hear . . .
So, no matter how downhearted
   And discouraged we may be,
New hope is born when we behold
   Leaves budding on a tree . . .
Or when we see a timid flower
   Push through the frozen sod
And open wide in glad surprise
   Its petaled eyes to God . . .
For this is just God saying,
   "Lift up your eyes to Me,
And the bleakness of your spirit,
   Like the budding springtime tree,
Will lose its wintry darkness
   And your heavy heart will sing"–
For God never sends the Winter
Without the joy of Spring.

Helen Steiner Rice

Used with permission of
The Helen Steiner Rice Foundation
Suite 2100 Atrium Two
221 E. Fourth Street
Cincinnati, OH 45202

The Healing Power
of Prayer

In a peaceful sanctuary
Removed from worldly care,
One finds spiritual solace
In the healing power of prayer.
Like pure refreshing waters
We cleanse the heart and soul,
And wash away the sorrows
When God is in control.
Burdens become lighter
When to Him we pray,
And the outlook brighter
To cheer us on our way.

Elsie Natalie Brady

It's Up To You!

Have you made someone happy,
   or made someone sad,
What have you done with
   the day that you had?
God gave it to you
   to do just as you would.
Did you do what was wicked,
   or do what was good?
Did you hand out a smile,
   or just give 'em a frown?
Did you lift someone up,
   or push someone down?
Did you lighten some load,
   or some progress impede?
Did you look for a rose,
   or just gather a weed?
What did you do with
   your beautiful day?
God gave it to you,
   did you throw it away?

The Great Caretaker

The caretaker in the garden,
Dedicated soul is he,
Who tills among the flowers
And toils among the trees.
He plants for simple pleasures,
In which he puts great store,
His gifts are garland flowers,
A wealth of waking chores.
He prunes and waters daily,
Among his hosts instills,
His congregation knows him,
The coffers all are filled.
His sermon is his flowers,
They stand for all he is,
And he finds peace among them,
Where the Great Caretaker lives.

Nancy Gill Halstenberg

44

A Living Faith

I'VE DREAMED many dreams that never came true,
   I've seen them vanish at dawn.
But I've realized enough of my dreams, thank God,
   To make me want to dream on.

I'VE PRAYED many prayers when no answer came
   Though I waited patient and long,
But answers have come to enough of my prayers
   To make me keep praying on.

I'VE TRUSTED many a friend that failed,
   And left me to weep alone.
But I've found enough of my friends true blue,
   To make me keep trusting on.

I'VE SOWN many seeds that fell by the way
   For the birds to feed upon,
But I've held enough golden sheaves in my hands
   To make me keep sowing on.

I'VE DRAINED the cup of disappointment and pain
   And gone many days without song,
But I've sipped enough nectar from the roses of life,
   To make me want to live on.

What Would You Give?

What would you give for a day in Spring,
With bright green grass and windy hills,
Sapphire skies and cotton clouds,
And the fairy gold of daffodils?
What would you give for a Summer day,
With your own rainbow overhead,
Butterflies and hummingbirds,
Hovering over each flower bed?

What would you give for an Autumn day,
With leaves of orange and brown and gold,
The smell of wood smoke in the air,
And all of the love your heart could hold?
What would you give for a Winter day,
Whose landscapes glisten white with snow,
A blazing fire and a friend to share
Sweet memories of long ago?

Is there among us anyone,
With wealth enough to purchase all
This loveliness, no human hand
Can duplicate, however small?
What do you suppose the price
And value of such things would be?
No man who lives is rich enough,
. . . To buy what God gives us FOR FREE!

Grace E. Easley

I Don't Know About Tomorrow . . .

I don't know about tomorrow,
What may come along the way;
I only know that God is with me,
And will help me face today . . .

I don't know about tomorrow,
Or remember all that's past,
But God will grant me strength
   and courage,
And make each precious moment last . . .

I don't know about tomorrow;
What new things may lie in store,
But I know that God will lead me,
As He's always done before . . .

I don't know about tomorrow,
But God will hold me in His hand;
He will fill me with His blessings,
And will help me understand!!!

                     Hope C. Oberhelman

Spring
Comes Every Year

Spring came to the valley
At sunup today,
And melted the snows in
An artistic way.
It lifted the leaves from
Each shell-covered bud
And smiled when it saw the
Narcissi in nod.

Spring came to the valley
When dawn filled the sky
And opened the eyelid of
Each sleeping eye.
It tinted the grass with
Chlorophyll green
And warmly embraced the
Ice-covered stream.

Spring came to the valley,
It comes every year;
If we will but harken,
God's message we'll hear:
The winter is past,
Rejoice all and sing;
The earth is alive with
The coming of spring.

Loise Pinkerton Fritz

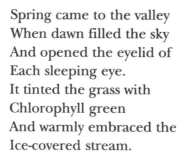

The Beautiful Rose

Flowers in abundance, the Master has made,
Beautiful colors, all on parade,
Sweet peas and Daisies and Arbutus too,
All diffuse fragrance for me and for you.

Violets and Four O'clocks, what an array!
Petunias and Pansies to brighten our day.
Dogwoods and Lilacs and Daffodils too,
And notice the Irises before we get through.

Heavenly Blues and Hollyhocks tall,
For our enjoyment, God made them all.
Carnations and Poppies and on the list goes,
But nothing can rival the Beautiful Rose.

Lester E. Bartholomew

A Rose Among Thorns

Sometimes, Lord, I'm like a rose
And the radiance within shines bright,
But other times I'm like a thorn
And dark as winter's night.

But, Lord, you know the who and when,
The why and what and where,
You know that deep inside each rose
The Source within does care.

And though at times the rose may shine
Have no fear for the thorn,
For He weaved them both together
And thus the rose was born.

He knew that both were needed
If in brilliance we're to stand,
So let the rose shine brightly
For the thorn is in His hand.

So don't ever doubt or wonder
About the bitter-sweet,
For God the great designer
Is the author of this treat.

So if at times we're shining
Or maybe sometimes dim,
Let's go quickly to the Author
And just give this rose to Him.

Chris Zambernard

A Little Sermon

You claim to have a Gospel
   to lead me on my way?
Remember, teach your message
   by what you do – not say.

Don't give me little pamphlets
   with words and pictures bright
Remember, your example
   is what gives spirits light.

Each time you try to tell me
   how good life ought to be –
Remember, I'll remember
   the good that I can see.

And when you raise your question
   about Eternity –
Remember who remembers
   how good you've been to me.

Eugene G. E. Botelho

God's Reason

I don't know how to say it,
But, somehow it seems to me
That maybe we are stationed,
Where God wants us to be.

That little place we're filling
Is the reason for our birth,
And just to do the work we do
He sent us down to earth.

If God had wanted otherwise,
I reckon he'd have made
Each one of us a little different
Of a worse or better grade.

And since God knows and understands
All things of land and sea,
I fancy that he placed us here,
Just where he wanted us to be.

Sometimes we get to thinking
As our labors we review,
That we should like a higher place
With greater things to do.

But we come to the conclusion,
When the envying is stilled,
That the post to which God sent us
Is the post He wanted filled.

Time Immortal

There's a time to live, a time to die,
A time for laughter and to cry.
Time is endless as can be
So much unlike both you and me.

Our time is measured by the Lord
And He alone can cut the cord.
We must make use of each new day
And tarry not along the way.

Give to all a helping hand,
Try to make them understand
That God has put us here on earth
To please Him and to show our worth.

Then as our life on earth runs out,
If Christians we have been devout,
So, too, our time will endless be
With God throughout eternity.

Albert Norman Theel

Life's Pathways

We know life has its moments
Of heartaches and despair,
And when we need a helping hand
We find God always there.

Life, too, is filled with joy and hope
That thrills us through and through,
And we should offer thanks to God
Day after day anew.

Life knows success and happiness,
Misfortune and distress.
In times like these with faith in God
We find true happiness.

Harold F. Mohn

We Must Matter

We must matter to each other–
　　Or we matter, not at all–
For the Lord bequeathed us kinship
　　To befriend each other's fall.
When a heart cries out in hunger
　　Or a pauper weeps in pain,
It must matter, to our kinship,
　　That they do not cry in vain.

We must help the soul who struggles
　　Through a trying time in life;
We must help the one who flounders
　　In some agony of strife;
It must be our Christian duty
　　To pay heed to every cry
And deny no soul the kindness
　　Of some need we can supply.

We could be the weeping pauper
　　Who is lonesomed by despair;
We could be the voice of hunger–
　　If we had the pain to bear–
So, we must pay heed and substance
　　To the needs of every plea
For– the voice that cries tomorrow–
　　Could belong to you or me.

We must not ignore the stranger
　　Who, in passing, staggers by;
We must not deny the beggar–
　　Or the aged, feeble cry,
For, our Lord gave love and kinship
　　To endear each heart, within–
And He made us all to matter
　　To each other and to Him.

　　　　　　　　　Michael Dubina

Along Life's Pathways

Happiness is like a crystal,
  Fair and exquisite and clear,
Broken in a million pieces,
  Scattered far and near.
Now and then along life's pathway,
  Lo, some shining fragments fall,
But there are so many pieces,
  No one ever finds them all.

You may find a bit of beauty,
  Or an honest share of wealth,
While another just beside you
  Gathers honor, love or health.

Vain to choose or grasp unduly,
    Broken is the perfect ball,
And there are so many pieces,
    No one ever finds them all.

Yet the wise, as on they journey,
    Treasure every fragment clear;
Fit them as they may together,
    Imagining the shattered sphere,
Learning ever to be thankful,
    Though their share of it be small,
For it has so many pieces,
    No one ever finds them all.

59

My Little Hill

There is a hill outside of town,
Not very far from here,
On which the pines grow thick and tall,
And beautiful all year!
It lies far from the other hills,
Secluded and alone,
I go there sometimes when I'm sad,
That hill is all my own.

I stand upon the very top,
Quite hidden by the trees;
I look out at the countryside,
And listen to the breeze.

There's something very restful,
In the stillness that I find,
And little cares and worries,
Sort of vanish from my mind.

The little hurts, the little pains,
My spirit could not drop,
All seem to disappear from me,
When I have reached the top.
And every heart should sometimes go,
Where all is quiet and still,
Life's road is not so weary,
When you have . . . A little Hill!

Grace E. Easley

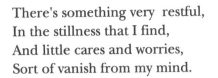

Within My Valley

Lord, I'm content with morning sun
And soft darkness when day is done,
Tallest pines swaying on the hills,
Meadow daisies and daffodils.

Lord, I'm thankful for gifts of love,
Like painted blueness in sky above–
All the beauty my heart can hold
Is in the days You weave of gold.

You send the breezes dancing free–
They kiss green leaves upon the tree
Then frolic off to swelling field
To sip a taste from friendly rill.

From all the places I have been
I now return to tranquil glen.
This is the place I feel Your touch–
Lord, You have given me so much.

Rosa Nelle Anderson

In His Footsteps

When someone does a kindness
   It always seems to me
That's the way God up in heaven
   Would like us all to be …
For when we bring some pleasure
   To another human heart,
We have followed in His footsteps
   And we've had a little part
In serving Him who loves us—
   For I am very sure it's true
That in serving those around us
   We serve and please Him, too.

Helen Steiner Rice

Used with permission of
The Helen Steiner Rice Foundation
Suite 2100 Atrium Two
221 E. Fourth Street
Cincinnati, OH 45202

God Bless You Always

May God bless you always, forever I pray,
Protect you while sleeping, and all through the day.
May He stand beside you, come sunset or dawn,
And His be the strength, you're depending upon.

May God bless you always, wherever you go,
Calming your fears, and helping you grow.
Soothing your heartaches, sharing your smiles,
And just being near, to lighten the miles.

May God bless you always, through sunlight and rain.
Always forgiving, again and again.
Teaching you patience, when things turn out wrong,
The value of hope, and the joy of a song.

May He be the friend, you never need doubt,
As He helps you discover what life's all about.
May He walk beside you, the rest of your days,
And I earnestly pray that God bless you always!

                                        Grace E. Easley

I Thank God,
for My Day

For the beauty of the morning
As I look across the field;
For the promise of the hour
As my thoughts to Him I yield.
For the work that lies before me,
And the things that need be done–
For refreshing rest of nighttime,
And the rising of the sun.

For the good I see in others,
And the kindness that they show
For the day that lies before me,
And the blessings that I know.
For a spirit that is lifted,
And a heart repent to pray . . .
For the joy I have this morning,
Is the song I sing all day.

All the troubles that surround me
Have no fear to take command.
For I have faith in Jesus,
Only He can understand.

Roxie Lusk Smith

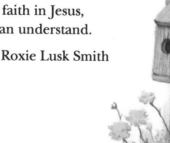

From Darkness Into Light

Thank you, Lord, for loving me
   when I didn't love myself,
Alone, unnoticed like a book
   on a long forgotten shelf.

Thank you, Lord, for showing me
   a new and better way.
You gave me hope so I could cope
   with problems of the day.

You dried my tears so I could see
   beyond my darkest night
The shadow of an empty tomb
   aglow in bright sunlight.

You lifted me when I was down;
   You heard my feeble prayer
And let me know that I was loved
   and worthy of repair.

Thank you, Lord, for all these things
   so beautiful and bright,
For taking time to change my life
   from darkness into light.

Clay Harrison

Miracles

At times life's little miracles
  are few and far between,
And yet they happen everyday
  though many go unseen.

May not be of great importance,
  no headline-seeking news,
Small mysteries to ponder on
  which often change our views.

A kindly word that brings a smile,
  a get-well card you send;
A letter from a loving son,
  a visit from a friend.

This renewal of our spirit, and
  release from stress and strain
Are miracles God works each day
  to make us whole again.

Angie Monnens

His Company

Alone but never lonely
Is a priceless gift I treasure
We all possess this gift of love
That is given in full measure.

But some I'm sure are unaware
As once I used to be
That deep within each soul abides
His loving company.

But once we are awakened
From our deep and dormant sleep
We begin at once to notice
A soul that's filled with peace.

Never more will you be lonely
For His company you'll treasure
'Tis a gift He gave to all of us
And given in full measure.

Never more will you be lonely
For now you recognize
That He is always with you
And you have won the Prize.

                Chris Zambernard

Magic of Blessings

Let me share, with you, my blessings
    That are joys within my heart
And behold a Heaven's magic
    That will multiply their lot
For, each time I share my blessings,
    God will double them, anew–
When you share them with another–
    Like I shared them all with you.

Let me give you of the harvest
    That is blessed upon my field;
Let me give you– from my larder–
    Of the best it has to yield
For there is a joy in giving
    That has holy magic, too,
And it multiplies my gladness
    For each joy I give to you.

There are also special blessings
    For each kindness I bestow–
Like the blessings of my harvests
    From the seeds I plant and sow–
But my best reward from Heaven,
    For my Christian deeds each day,
Is the way God doubles blessings
    That I share or give away.

                    Michael Dubina

You Are the One

You are the one who has to decide
    Whether you'll do it or toss it aside,
You are the one who makes up your mind
    Whether you'll lead or linger behind.

Whether you'll try for the goal that's afar
    Or be contented to stay where you are.
Take it or leave. Here's something to do,
    Just think it over. It's all up to you!

What do you wish? To be known as a shirk
    Or known as someone who's willing to work,
Scorned for a loafer or praised by your chief
    Rich or poor, beggar or thief?

Eager or earnest or dull through the day,
    Honest or crooked? It's you who must say!
You must decide in the face of the test
    Whether you'll shirk it or give your best.

My Own Path

The way behind is dark,
    O Lord,
No light ahead
    I see.

Give me the faith
    that guides me on,
And trust,
    that follows Thee.

Roxie Lusk Smith

In Him Fully Trust

In times of want and trouble
Why do we turn to God,
While during bright and shiny
    days
We give Him just a nod?
He wants to be our constant
    Guide,
To daily walk with us;
Then let us yield ourselves
    to Him
And in Him fully trust.

Loise Pinkerton Fritz
(Psalm 62:8)

From the Vision Splendid

'Mid all the traffic of the ways,
Turmoils without, within,
Make in my heart a quiet place,
And come and dwell therein:

A little shrine of quietness,
All sacred to Thyself,
Where Thou shalt all my soul possess,
And I may find myself:

A little shelter from life's stress,
Where I may lay me prone,
And bare my soul in loneliness,
And know as I am known:

A little place of mystic grace,
Of self and sin swept bare,
Where I may look upon Thy face,
And talk with Thee in prayer.

John Oxenham

Dear Jesus

Who was the baby born of old,
Within a manger dark and cold,
Of Virgin Mother as foretold?
. . . Dear Jesus!
Who raised the dead and cured the lame,
Blessing everyone who came,
Always in His Father's Name?
. . . Dear Jesus!

Who sadly said it would be so,
Before the cock three times would crow,
That one would say he did not know
. . . Dear Jesus?
Nailed high upon the bitter tree,
Who heard the good thief's dying plea,
With "Thou shalt this day be with Me"?
. . . Dear Jesus!

And by Whose dear lips was it said,
He truly would rise from the dead,
Bringing life to all instead?
. . . Dear Jesus!
Who is it stands without and knocks,
Stills the storm when our boat rocks,
Is the safest of all docks?
. . . Dear Jesus!

And who has promised we should be
With Him through eternity,
If we live our lives as He?
. . . Dear Jesus!
Dear Lord, please grant that never I
Should ever doubt or question why,
Breathing one name ere I die,
. . . " DEAR JESUS"!

Grace E. Easley

Home

A home is the dream
  Of a husband and wife,
To share with their children
  On their journey thru life.

A home comes alive
  With love and good cheer,
Enriching the lives
  Of those it holds dear.

It grows with you, comforts you
  And gives quiet joy,
It nurtures the childhood
  Of each girl or boy.

Its rooms can hold special
    Attractions for you,
Where the sun seems to shine
    A bit brighter for you.

With sweet heaven's blessings
    Each day of the year,
Our home is our refuge
    From life's threats or fears.

The years come and go
    And the children may roam,
But they always return–
    For there's no place like home.

            Catherine Janssen Irwin

The Streets of Circumstance

Upon the streets of circumstance
    each day we meet a few
Who have no safe abiding place
    and dreams that won't come true.
With heads held high, most pass them by
    indifferent to their pain.
They hurry by and do not speak
    to beggars in the rain.
As hands reach out, they turn away
    pretending not to see
The broken hearts before their eyes
    in a mask of misery.
Where do they sleep when nights are cold
    and spring is far away
Upon the streets of circumstance
    before the light of day?
Is there no place for them to go;
    is there no one to care
For the least of these, God's children,
    who are dying everywhere?
In the land of milk and honey
    why must so many die ...
Upon the streets of circumstance
    would Jesus pass them by?

                Clay Harrison

God's Tender, Loving Grace

Each rocky road, each winding stair
Has known His blessed presence there;
The wildest storm, the roughest sea
With His sweet grace, no threat could be.

His arms enfold me through the night
Until the dawn comes into sight;
His tender mercy and love abide
As I cast doubt and fear aside.

He comforts me when hope runs thin
And loves me if I lose or win;
So when I find I need a friend
I know my Lord, my cares will mend.

Catherine Janssen Irwin

In Touch

I say a thousand little prayers
   Throughout my busy day.
I keep in touch with Jesus
   In my simple little way.

Sometimes it's merely, "thank you,"
   Or I praise His holy name.
Yet He showers me with blessings,
   He loves me just the same.

My friend, it's not the longest prayer
   Or whether you're on your knees.
He wants to know He's on your mind,
   These are the things that please.

So, keep in touch with Jesus,
   Reach out for His helping hand.
For He's ever so close beside you,
   Like the footprints in the sand.

              Helen Parker

Winter Woods

I grew up in this forest and I knew
These giant trees when they were nothing more
Than slender saplings swaying in the wind;
Sought solitude, delighted in the lore
Of nature, who became my teacher first;
Walked down trails where sun and shadows meet,
Through silence softly tucked about the days;
Traced the twists and turns of every creek.
Stepping lightly through the after-glow,
Amid the falling flakes of silver white,
Belonging to the moment and the mood,
Another little creature of the night,
With quickened breath and ears attuned, who stood
. . . Sensing God within this winter wood!

Grace E. Easley

God Transcends All Things

I glimpse Your beauty in each gorgeous rainbow
And feel Your Presence near each fragrant rose;
I hear Your voice re-echo in the woodland
And discern Your touch in every breeze that blows.

Your radiant Face I find in crimson sunsets.
Your perfection shines down on moonlit streams,
Your majesty's portrayed by purple mountains
And from stars Your love comes down in silvery beams.

I sense your grace in every dewdrop,
Your glory in glistening snow upon the trees,
Your Providence feeds birds and clothes the lilies–
God, how wonderful Your love transcends all these!

Sister Mary Gemma Brunke

Keep A-goin'

If you strike a thorn or rose,
   Keep a-goin'!
If it hails or if it snows,
   Keep a-goin'!
'Taint no use to sit an' whine
When the fish ain't on your line;
Bait your hook an' keep a-tryin'–
   Keep a-goin'!

When the weather kills your crop,
   Keep a-goin'!
Though 'tis work to reach the top,
   Keep a-goin'!
S'pose you're out o' ev'ry dime,
Gittin' broke ain't any crime;
Tell the world you're feelin' *prime*–
   Keep a-goin'!

When it looks like all is up,
   Keep a-goin'!
Drain the sweetness from the cup,
   Keep a-goin'!
See the wild birds on the wing,
Hear the bells that sweetly ring,
When you feel like sighin', sing–
Keep a-goin'!

       Frank L. Stanton

Value Every Day

A day without love is a cold, cold day
When worldly riches fade away.

A day without hope is a dreary day
Filled with shadows of dismay.

A day without faith is a fruitless day
As we trudge along life's way.

A day without friends is a lonely day
Without a cheery word to say.

Embracing faith, hope and love
Assures sweet blessings from above.

Catherine Janssen Irwin

Hope

So frail a thing– and yet how strong!
　So heartening when things go wrong!
In fear and darkness we may grope
But how it clears when we find Hope!

It's always there, a cheerful friend,
Prepared its courage vast to lend
　To those who feel they cannot win.
　To find it merely raise your chin.

Just look aloft and from the skies
As if it came from God's own eyes,
　You'll gather strength with life to cope.
　You'll taste the poor man's nectar– Hope!

Success and failure are not real.
Hope for the things that life can't steal!

Nick Kenny

Give Us This Day

The sun has lulled the stars to sleep;
   another day's begun.
The sky reflects His majesty
   beyond the morning sun.

Give us this day, dear Lord,
   to rise and shine for you.
May we reflect the kingdom here
   in everything we do.

If we should stray, guide us, Lord,
   down righteous paths today,
And shine through us Thy holy light
   like moonlight on the bay.

Show us, too, a better way
   to serve as you would do . . .
Give us this day, dear Lord,
   to live and work for You.

Clay Harrison

Happiness

Happy is he who by love's sweet song,
Is cheered today as he goes along.
Happier is he, who believes that
   tomorrow
Will ease the pain and take away
   sorrow.
Happiest, he, who on earthly sod
Has faith in himself, his friends
   and God.

Where the Wildflowers Grow

Out in the fields where
The wildflowers grow
And the wisp of the wind
Sways the blooms to and fro,
There's a beauty that lets
Only sweet thoughts unfold ...
Out in the fields where
The wildflowers grow.

Out in the fields where
The wildflowers grow
And the song of the birds
Like a melody flows,
There's a peace God bestows
That brings joy to the soul ...
Out in the fields where
The wildflowers grow.

Loise Pinkerton Fritz

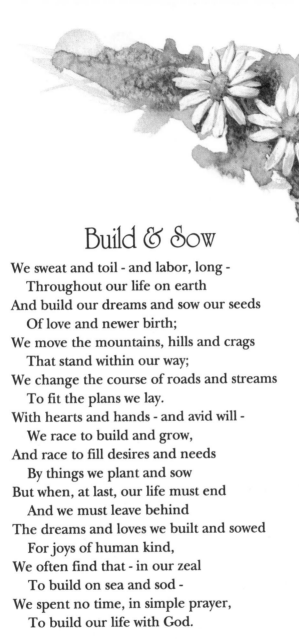

Build & Sow

We sweat and toil - and labor, long -
　　Throughout our life on earth
And build our dreams and sow our seeds
　　Of love and newer birth;
We move the mountains, hills and crags
　　That stand within our way;
We change the course of roads and streams
　　To fit the plans we lay.
With hearts and hands - and avid will -
　　We race to build and grow,
And race to fill desires and needs
　　By things we plant and sow
But when, at last, our life must end
　　And we must leave behind
The dreams and loves we built and sowed
　　For joys of human kind,
We often find that - in our zeal
　　To build on sea and sod -
We spent no time, in simple prayer,
　　To build our life with God.

Michael Dubina

Silent Prayer

What a beautiful day this is, Lord,
My happy heart has wings.
I feel so very close to You,
And every bird that sings,
Echoes my own gratitude,
Because I have a part
In moments such as these, that are
Engraved upon my heart.

There never was a bluer sky,
Or more delightful breeze,
As little sunbeams filter through
The branches of the trees.
The scent of pine and cedar
Lies thick upon the air,
As Autumn weaves a magic almost
More than I can bear.

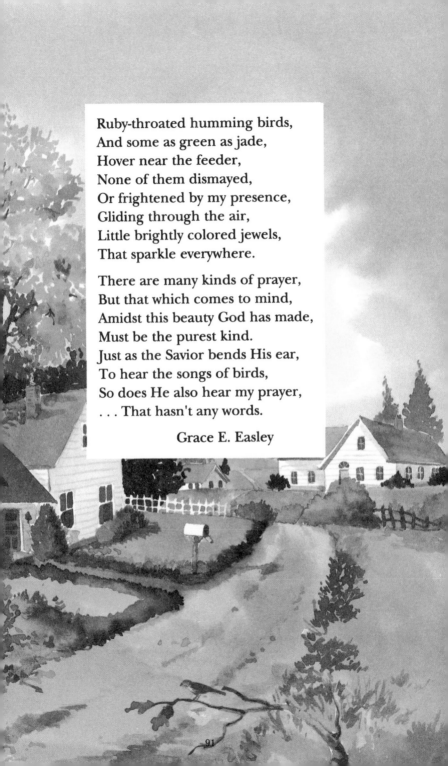

Ruby-throated humming birds,
And some as green as jade,
Hover near the feeder,
None of them dismayed,
Or frightened by my presence,
Gliding through the air,
Little brightly colored jewels,
That sparkle everywhere.

There are many kinds of prayer,
But that which comes to mind,
Amidst this beauty God has made,
Must be the purest kind.
Just as the Savior bends His ear,
To hear the songs of birds,
So does He also hear my prayer,
. . . That hasn't any words.

Grace E. Easley

Stairway to Heaven

The stairway to Heaven
  Is what we should seek,
And never stop climbing
  Till we reach the peak.

The going seems easy
  First couple of stairs –
We're young with the Lord
  And free from most cares.

But then as we climb
  Thru the years of our life,
We're slowed down a bit
  By heartaches and strife.

A step or two backwards
  As our faith starts to dim,
Then surging on upwards
  As we're lifted by Him.

One day we will reach
  The top of the stairs,
God's Kingdom at last
  With Him we will share.

Albert Norman Theel

He Walks Beside

I walked a sunlit mountain path,
My Savior walked along;
And there 'mid heaven's blue and gold
He filled my heart with song.
I walked a rugged valley trail, afraid.
The way grew dim;
Then Jesus reached and took my hand,
I found new strength in Him.
In every circumstance of life
Be skies bright blue or grey,
He walks beside me and His grace
Sustains me all the way.

Beverly J. Anderson

Treasures

Out of this life I shall never take
Things of silver and gold I make.
All that I cherish and hoard away
After I leave, on this earth must stay.
Tho' I have toiled for a painting rare
To hang on the wall, I must leave it there.
Tho' I call it mine, and boast its worth,
I must give it up when I leave this earth.
All that I gather, and all that I keep
I must leave behind when I fall asleep.

And I often wonder what I shall own
In that other life, when I pass alone.
What shall they find, and what
Shall they see, in the soul that
Answers the call for me?
Shall the Great Judge learn
When my task is through,
That my spirit has gathered some riches
    too?
Or shall at last it be mine to find
That all I'd worked for I'd left behind.

A Spiritual Path

I never walk alone,
afraid;
A path before me,
God, has made.
I never yield to fear
and force:
God keeps me on
A steady course.

Roxie Lusk Smith

Life's Inner Worth

There is no path worth while
Upon the face of earth
Unless man knows sweet peace
And life's true inner worth.
For strength will come each mile
When weary steps grow faint
And faith in God increase
With wisdom of a saint.

Loreta Inman

Castles in the Air

We all build castles in the air
For dreams are made of such,
We seek a rainbow or a star
In nature's friendly touch,
The sky of blue that beckons us
A springtime country lane,
We find the sunshine golden there
Right after April's rain.

Air castles are a joyous thing
For they are built of love,
And they are part of God's rich plan
This God who reigns above.

Tis He who helps our hearts to dream
And lends each bright ideal,
He helps our eyes to ever look
And find each glory real.

Till work is done we still shall build
And we shall seek our goal,
Then one day when the time is right
We'll find a richer role,
Foundations placed on firmer soil
And life so much more fair,
When dreams come true we bring to earth
Our castles in the air.

Garnett Ann Schultz

My Whole Life Long

My whole life long seems very short,
However many years.
I've had a lot of happy times,
And cried a lot of tears.
I thought I'd be forever young,
But then lo and behold,
I looked into the mirror,
And discovered I was old.

But that is how it's meant to be,
Beyond this earth I know,
God has reserved a better place,
For you and I to go.
No sickness and no sorrow,
Will Heaven's walls contain,
And every blessed one of us,
. . . Shall be brand new again.

Grace E. Easley

Upstream

The easy roads are crowded, and
  The level roads are jammed.
The pleasant little rivers
  With the drifting folks are crammed.
But off yonder where it's rocky,
  Where you get the better view,
You will find the ranks are thinning,
  And the travelers are few.

Where the going's smooth and pleasant
  You will always find the throng,
For the many– more's the pity–
  Seem to like to drift along.
But the steeps that call for courage
  And the task that's hard to do
In the end results in glory
  For the never wavering few!

Love is Forever

Love is not some fragile thing
    that parting can somehow sever.
Love that's true dwells within
    Living on and on forever.

Through the years, love sincere
    Grows stronger day by day.
Though the one who is dearly loved
    May be many miles away.

A certain word or a special song,
    Though memories oft' grow dim,
Love will suddenly stir the soul
    And come rushing back again.

Gladys Adkins

*I thank my God upon every
remembrance of you. (Phil. 1:3)*

To the Quitter

The world won't care if you quit
And the world won't whine if you fail
The busy world won't notice it,
No matter how loudly you wail.

Nobody will worry that you
Have relinquished the fight
And gone down
For it's only the things that you do
That are worth while and get your renown.

The quitters are quickly forgot
Of them the world spends little time
And a few e'er care that you've not
The courage or patience to climb.

So give up and quit in despair,
And take your place back on the shelf
But don't think the world's going to care;
You are injuring only yourself.

The Edge of Loneliness

I seek the Edge of Loneliness,
Where few have dared to trod,
Wherein the mystic stillness bids
Me keep my tryst with God.

Like winged bird, my soul takes flight,
Unfettered, wild, and free
To search beyond all earthly thought
To find Eternity.

Drifting, then, on Winds of Time,
With nought to break the flight
Of silvered wings, I seek my God
Above all alpine height.

I seek the Edge of Loneliness,
Transcending Time and Space,
To where my soul communes with God ...
And meets Him Face-to-face.

Sister Miriam Barker, C.D.S.

Each Day Brings
a Chance to Do Better

How often we wish for another chance
    to make a fresh beginning,
A chance to blot out our mistakes
    and change failure into winning–
And it does not take a special time
    to make a brand-new start,
It only takes the deep desire
    to try with all our heart
To live a little better
    and to always be forgiving
And to add a little "sunshine"
    to the world in which we're living–
So never give up in despair
    and think that you are through,
For there's always a tomorrow
    and a chance to start anew.

Helen Steiner Rice

Used with permission of
The Helen Steiner Rice Foundation
Suite 2100 Atrium Two
221 E. Fourth Street
Cincinnati, OH 45202

The Good Life

The good life is more
than just being happy;
It's helping to make
someone else happy, too.
The good life is more
than achieving success;
It's helping another to
reach his goals, too.

The good life is more
than just having talents;
It's using our talents
to help fellow man.

The good life is more
Than just being healthy;
It's helping less
fortunates all we can.

The good life is more
than just having plenty;
It's seeing that others
get their fair share, too.
The good life means more
than loving Lord Jesus;
It's helping others
to know Him, too.

Ruth Scarbrough

God's Choice

God made the earth and heaven
Each for a purpose meant,
For us all He gave His life
For us all His blood was spent.

He made the weeds to ramble,
He made some flowers rare,
But He gives to all, the showers
And the sun, shines everywhere.

He sees our every action,
He knows our every need.
There's no adding or subtraction
And Love His only creed.

He loves the rich, He loves the poor,
There is no distinction there
An be you rich or be you poor,
He loves to hear your prayer.

Daniel F. O'Connell

The Handle of the Heart

There is a door to every heart,
And yet alas, my friend,
There's but a single handle,
And that one is within.
The outside is not fitted,
With any lock or key,
And though the Lord may stand
   and knock,
The rest is up to thee.

How many lonely hours,
Each one of us has known,
Who would not let Him enter,
And preferred to be alone.
How many needless sorrows,
We all have had to bear,
Who would not open up our hearts,
And left Him standing there.

Years have a way of passing,
Like the blinking of an eye,
It seems we are no sooner born,
…Before we have to die.
Treasured moments are as but
The flicker of a candle,
But Heaven can be won with just
…The lifting of a handle.

              Grace E. Easley

On Friendship

It's love that makes
the world go 'round,
And love is based
on friendship sound;
If everyone
would be a friend
To everyone until the end,
then fear and strife
would hide away
And harmony would rule the day.

Pearl E. Auer

The Friend Who Just Stands By

When trouble comes your soul to try,
You love the friend who just stands by.
Perhaps there's nothing he can do;
The thing is strictly up to you,
For there are troubles all your own,
And paths the soul must tread alone;
Times when love can't smooth the road,
Nor friendship lift the heavy load.

But just to feel you have a friend,
Who will stand by until the end;
Whose sympathy through all endures,
Whose warm handclasp is always yours.
It helps somehow to pull you through,
Although there's nothing he can do;
And so with fervent heart we cry,
"God bless the friend who just stands by."

Garden of Life

In our days of life and journeys
    There is much that we must do
To endear ourselves to Jesus
    In this world we're passing through.
There are cares that we must render;
    There are loves that we must sow;
For our life, on earth, is measured
    By the good things we bestow.

We must make of life a garden
    That is covenant with our Lord
And must seed it with the virtues
    Of His doctrines and accords;
We must plant His seeds of mercy
    And must sow His love to share -
And each harvest that we gather,
    We must plant, anew, to bear.

Such a garden will be holy
　　To the Maker of the seeds
And will flower many blessings
　　For our Christian ways and deeds.
He will see we planted wisely -
　　Of the choices He affords -
And will bless us with a harvest
　　That returns its own rewards.

But we must not stop to revel
　　In the Graces that we win
For the Lord is ever needful
　　Of the loves that hinder sin.
We must cultivate more gardens
　　And must grow more love to share -
And be heart to heart with Jesus,
　　In our labors and our prayers.

　　　　　　　Michael Dubina

Trust In God

Love can blossom like a flower,
When our hearts turn to God.
Love stays with us every hour,
Though rough paths we must trod.

Love opens doors to happiness,
And God will show the way
To each believing follower
Who learns to trust and pray.

Mary H. Wittner

Not Alone

I cannot walk alone, dear Lord,
  Without the touch of Your hand.
My legs are weak and I'm afraid
  But I know You understand.

When I reach out for You, dear Lord,
  I always find You there.
And You will renew my strength
  When I come to You in prayer.

You've given me many blessings, Lord,
  Including a heart that sings.
And as I walk in Your shadow
  I am safe beneath Your wings.

In my distress I cried, dear Lord,
  And I know You heard my plea.
You said, "Dear child, take My hand,"
  And, "Fear not but come unto Me."

I know I need not fear, dear Lord,
  For You call me by my name.
You'll walk with me all the way
  And help me to not complain.

                    Gladys Adkins

For I the Lord thy God will
hold thy right hand, saying unto thee,
Fear not; I will help thee.
(Is2. 41:13)

When Trouble Comes
and Things Go Wrong!

Let us go quietly to God
   when troubles come to us,
Let us never stop to whimper
   or complain and fret and fuss,
Let us hide "our thorns" in "roses"
   and our sighs in "golden song"
And our "crosses" in a "crown of smiles"
   whenever things go wrong.
For no one can really help us
   as our troubles we bemoan,
For *comfort, help,* and *inner peace*
   must come from God alone.
So do not tell your neighbor,
   your companion, or your friend
In the hope that they can help you
   bring your troubles to an end,
For they, too, have their problems,
   they are burdened just like you,
So *take your cross to Jesus*
   and *He will see you through.*
And waste no time in crying
   on the shoulder of a friend
But go directly to the Lord
   for on Him you can depend.
For there's absolutely *nothing*
   that His mighty hand can't do
And He never is too busy
   to help and comfort you.

Helen Steiner Rice

Used with permission of
The Helen Steiner Rice Foundation
Suite 2100 Atrium Two
221 E. Fourth Street
Cincinnati, OH 45202

The Gift List

Put love at the top of your gift list,
For those who are so hard to please.
It's a present that all will enjoy,
And it can be given with ease.

Give kindness to those who are lonely,
And if this gift is returned,
Then you shall be surely rewarded,
For kindness should never be spurned.

Give attention to those who're not
    knowing
What it's like to be understood.
To help share another one's burden
Makes life really worthwhile and good.

Give praise to those who're down-trodden
With problems and cares of the day,
Uplifting words and a handshake
Will surely lighten their way.

Give courage to those who don't have it.
Give a smile instead of a frown.
This will help the one who is lonesome
To keep looking up and not down.

These gifts do not have any price tag.
Not a penny is the whole cost to you.
Yet, when they are all freely given
They will last your whole lifetime through.

*T*alk not of strength,
till your heart has known
And fought with weakness
through long hours alone.

Talk not of virtue,
till your conquering soul
has met temptation
and gained full control.

Boast not of garments,
all unscorched by sin,
Till you have passed unscathed
through fires within.

Follow Your Star

On the pathway of life
Your way may seem far,
But look to the sky
And follow your Star.

Whenever your life
Is touched by sorrow,
Your Star is there waiting
Through every tomorrow.

Though covered by clouds
On dark, dreary day,
Your Star will not leave -
Just bid it to stay.

And if you are weary,
And seek a release,
Your Star will bring comfort
And God's holy Peace.

Behind all life's shadows
Your Star will be there -
Just follow your Star,
For your Star's really ... PRAYER!

Sister Miriam Barker, C.D.S.

The Journey Back

This is a day for writing quiet things,
A peaceful stillness settles over me,
Wedged between the branches of a tree,
One small bird's-nest to which a feather clings,
Empty now of spotted eggs and wings.
A brown leaf falls in silent empathy,
And I recall how short a year can be,
Knowing the changes that a season brings.
This narrow trail leads past a rustic lodge,
How long it is since I have come this way,
But there are times one needs to be alone,
And these are woods I used to call my own,
Where first it was I knew God listens to
... A poet, with inmortal words to say.

Grace E. Easley

Entrustment

I ask Thy grace from day to day -
To live and work in gladsome way;
To yield my life as though it be
     the final step to eternity–
Help me obey the things You taught -
Be clean in action, pure in thought.
Take Thou, my heart and let it be
     admonished for eternity–
If living would demand its toll,
And strip from me, my very soul,
Forgive me, Lord, Thy glory be
     replenished for eternity–
You gave me breath - it's Yours to give;
Please know me, Lord! Each day I live,
Take Thou, my hand, and walk with me
     the final step to eternity–

          Roxie Lusk Smith

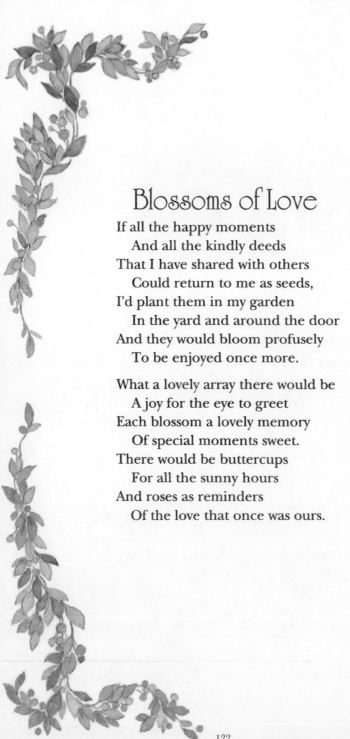

Blossoms of Love

If all the happy moments
　And all the kindly deeds
That I have shared with others
　Could return to me as seeds,
I'd plant them in my garden
　In the yard and around the door
And they would bloom profusely
　To be enjoyed once more.

What a lovely array there would be
　A joy for the eye to greet
Each blossom a lovely memory
　Of special moments sweet.
There would be buttercups
　For all the sunny hours
And roses as reminders
　Of the love that once was ours.

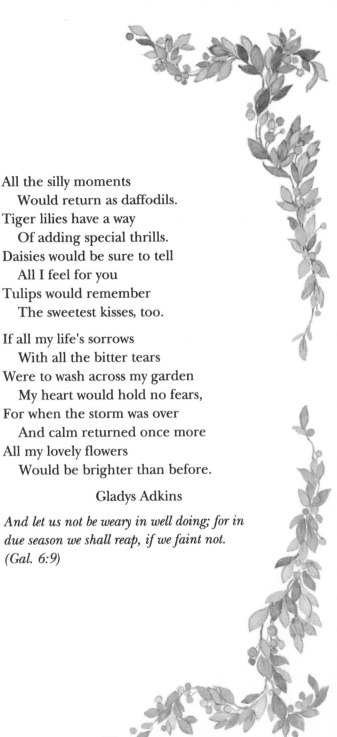

All the silly moments
    Would return as daffodils.
Tiger lilies have a way
    Of adding special thrills.
Daisies would be sure to tell
    All I feel for you
Tulips would remember
    The sweetest kisses, too.

If all my life's sorrows
    With all the bitter tears
Were to wash across my garden
    My heart would hold no fears,
For when the storm was over
    And calm returned once more
All my lovely flowers
    Would be brighter than before.

Gladys Adkins

And let us not be weary in well doing; for in due season we shall reap, if we faint not. (Gal. 6:9)

Standing Still

I never heard His whisper
nor felt His soft embrace.
I was far too busy running
a never ending race.

A race that kept me dancing
to a tune that wouldn't end.
So I never felt the soft caress
of my Eternal Friend.

The dance became more frantic
as the emptiness just grew.
I could not continue moving
to that familiar song I knew.

Exhausted from the running
and the dancing, oh so fast,
I simply stood and welcomed Him
while standing still at last.

Diane Denise Lake

A Better Gift

Mend a quarrel
Seek out a forgotten friend
Share some treasure
Give a soft answer
Encourage youth
Keep a promise
Find the time
Listen
Apologize if you were wrong
Be gentle
Laugh a little
Laugh a little more
Express your gratitude
Welcome a stranger
Gladden the heart of a child
Take pleasure in beauty and wonder of the earth
Speak your love
Speak it again
Speak it still once again

Time Out

There are many a rest on the side
of the road . . .
If we'd only pause for a moment,
To see the sun-laced lovely sky
then look to the world like you own it.

There you'll find comfort as you
pause, rest, and dream . . .
And laugh out loud with the world,
Then you can still your burden within
that a short while ago deep it stirred.

There are many a rest on the side of
the road . . .
Like a heavenly sanctuary
So be still and know
that your world can glow
And your burden no longer need carry.

So gaze beyond the threat of rain
and give thanks for this moment,
Then you can start your journey again
and look to the world like you own it.

Chris Zambernard

A Poet's Prayer

Let me not lose the wonder of
    this earth
When I become enmeshed in daily
    toil.
Open my ears to Springtime's
    joyous mirth,
My eyes behold the promise of
    the soil.
Let me remember quiet mountain
    heights,
Or dusk who folds her wings above
    the sea.
Awake to crystal dawn's first
    freshening lights,
These things made life so beautiful
    for me.
Give me the faith to see beyond
    all fears,
And wisdom for each trial that
    meets my day.
Teach me the words to halt my
    brother's tears,
And find the courage in truth's
    shining way.
Of all my prayers, Lord, grant me
    this one part,
The understanding of a loving heart.

            Zelma S. Dennis

The Power of God

God is a source of strength and hope
To face each new born day.
God like a beacon in the night
Will guide you on your way.

God never will refuse to lend
A helping hand to you.
God takes the darkness out of life
And lets the sun shine through.

God is the friend of everyone
No matter rich or poor.
God's words are those of truth and love
That ever will endure.

Harold F. Mohn